*easy* **BANJO TAB EDITION**

# JUST FOR FUN

# CLASSIC ROCK BANJO

## 12 GREAT SONGS OF THE '60s, '70s, & '80s

### ARRANGED BY ANDREW DUBROCK

T0053209

Produced by
Alfred Music Publishing Co., Inc.
P.O. Box 10003
Van Nuys, CA 91410-0003
alfred.com

Printed in USA.

ISBN-10: 0-7390-6459-2
ISBN-13: 978-0-7390-6459-7

Cover Photos

Central image models: Katrina Hruschka and Andrew Callahan / Photographer: Brian Immke, www.adeptstudios.com
Mastertone banjo: courtesy of Gibson USA • Moon: courtesy of The Library of Congress • Gramophone: © istockphoto / Faruk Tasdemir
MP3 player: © istockphoto / tpopova • Microphone: © istockphoto / Graffizone • Handstand: © istockphoto / jhorrocks
Jumping woman: © istockphoto / Dan Wilton • Woman and radio: courtesy of The Library of Congress • Sneakers: © istockphoto / ozgurdonmaz
Background: image copyright Elise Gravel, 2009, used under license from Shutterstock.com

 Contents printed on 100% recycled paper.

# FOREWORD

*Classic Rock Banjo* is designed for your total enjoyment.
Each song uses the original guitar parts arranged for the banjo,
and in some cases we've added banjo roll and picking patterns—
just for fun! Make sure to listen to the original recordings so you
know how the parts should sound before you start trying to learn
them. But most important, just have fun!

—Aaron Stang, Editor
Alfred Music Publishing Co., Inc.

# CONTENTS

# AFTER MIDNIGHT

Words and Music by
J.J. CALE

**Moderately fast rock**

*Intro:*

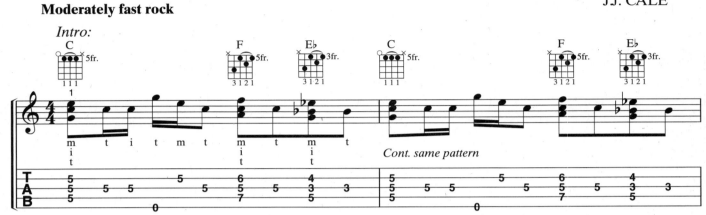

*Cont. same pattern*

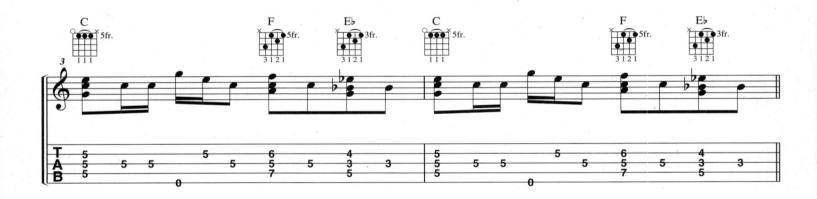

*Verse:*

1. Af - ter mid - night,_____ we gon' let it all___ hang___
2. Af - ter mid - night,_____ we gon' shake your tam - bou -

After Midnight - 3 - 1

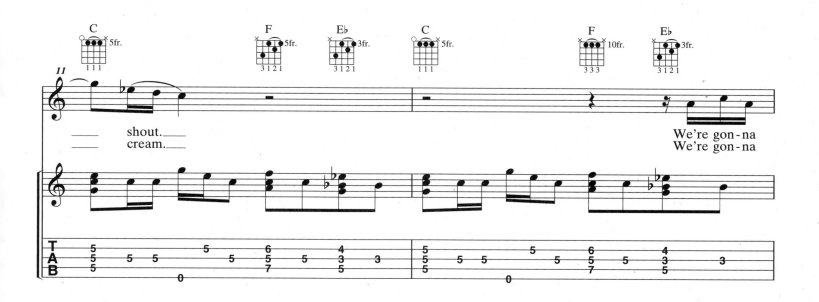

# GO YOUR OWN WAY

Words and Music by
LINDSEY BUCKINGHAM

⊕ *Coda*

**Chorus:**

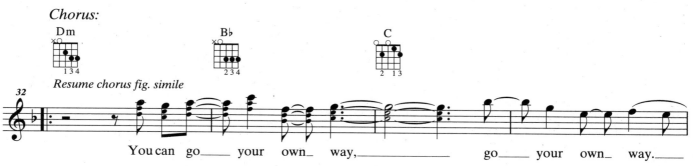

You can go___ your own___ way,_____ go___ your own___ way.___

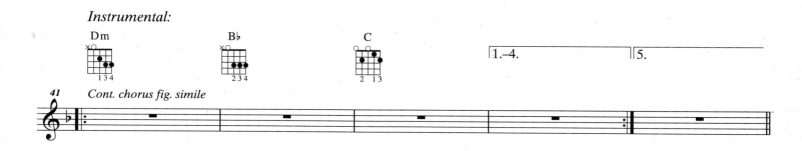

___ You can call___ it an - oth - er lone - ly day.___

**Instrumental:**

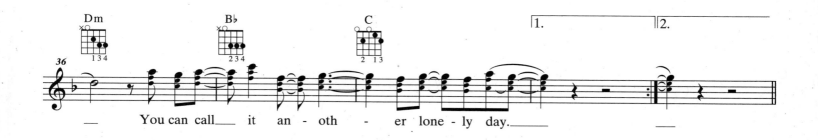

*Cont. chorus fig. simile*

**Chorus:**

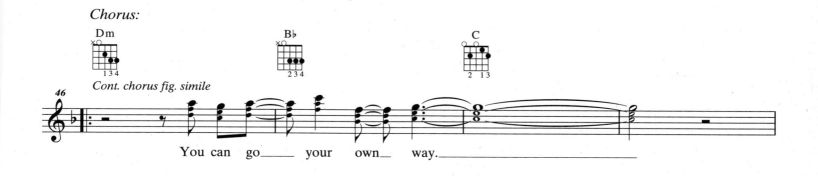

*Cont. chorus fig. simile*

You can go___ your own___ way.___

*Repeat and fade*

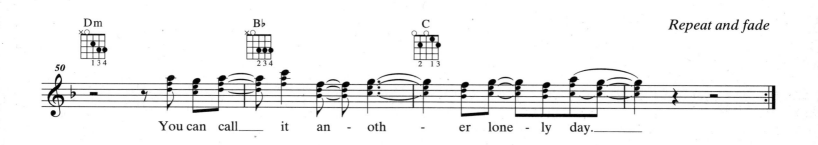

You can call___ it an - oth - er lone - ly day.___

# HOTEL CALIFORNIA

Words and Music by
DON HENLEY, GLENN FREY
and DON FELDER

Hotel California - 4 - 1

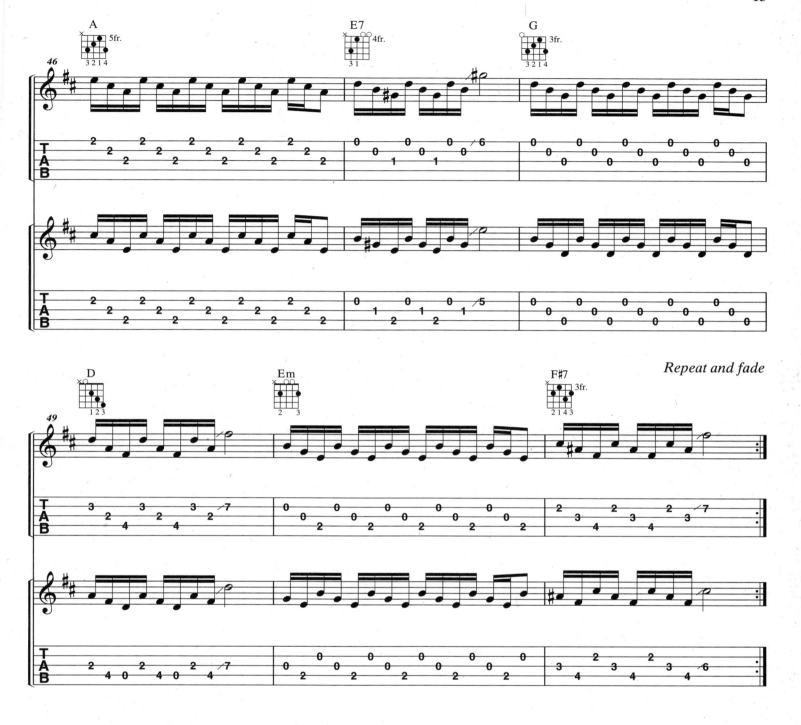

*Verse 3:*
Mirrors on the ceiling, the pink champagne on ice.
And she said, "We are all just prisoners here of our own device."
And in the master's chambers they gathered for the feast.
They stab it with their steely knives but they just can't kill the beast.
Last thing I remember I was running for the door.
I had to find the passage back to the place I was before.
"Relax," said the nightman, "We are programmed to receive."
You can check out anytime you like but you can never leave.

# IT'S ALL OVER NOW

Words and Music by
BOBBY and SHIRLEY WOMACK

It's All Over Now - 3 - 1

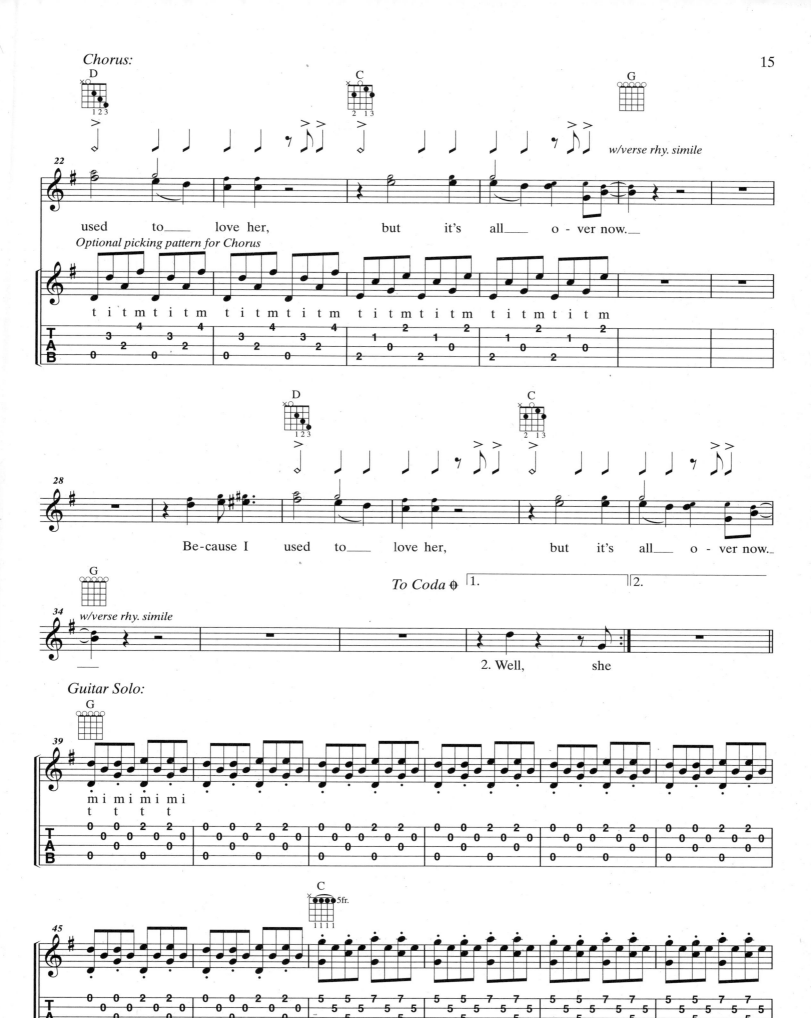

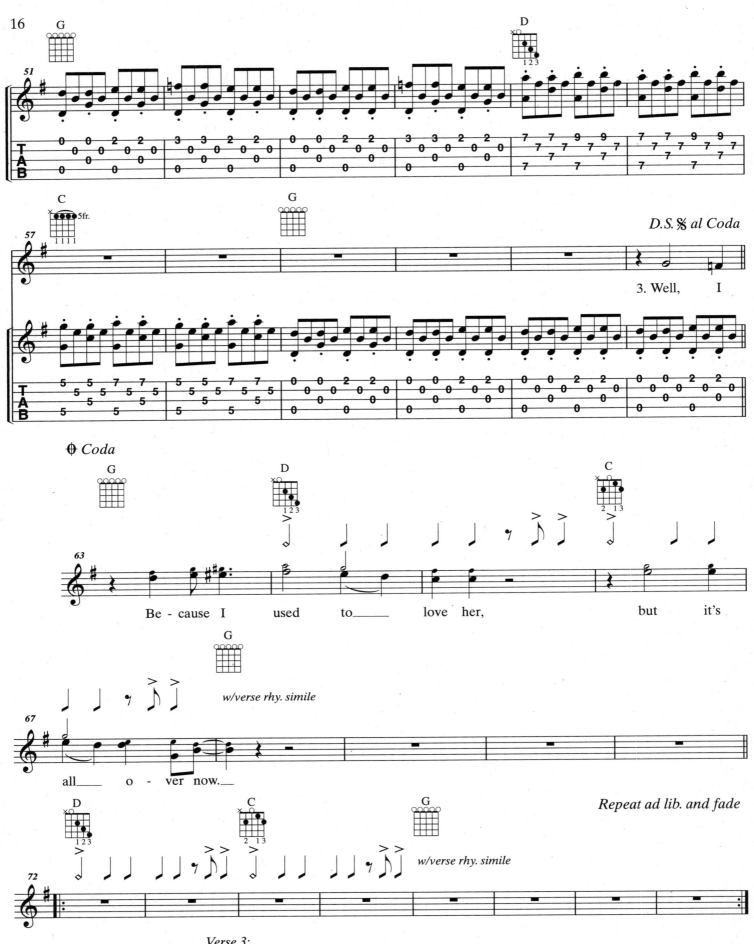

*Verse 3:*
Well, I used to wake in the morning, get my breakfast in bed.
When I'd gotten worried, she'd ease my aching head.
But now she's here and there with every man in town,
Still trying to take me for that same old clown.
*(To Chorus:)*

# LONG TRAIN RUNNIN'

D.S. % al Coda

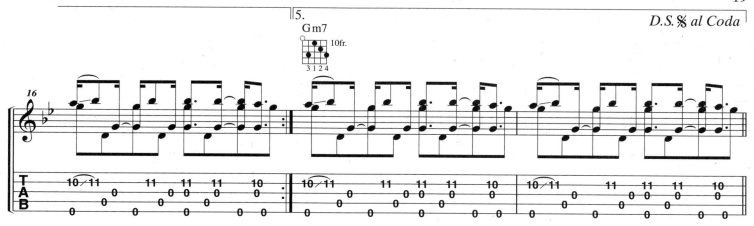

Verse 2:
You know I saw Miss Lucy,
Down along the tracks;
She lost her home and her family,
And she won't be comin' back.
Without love, where would you be right now,
Without love?

Verses 3 & 5:
Well, the Illinois Central
And the Southern Central freight,
Gotta keep on pushin', mama,
'Cause you know they're runnin' late.
Without love, where would you be right now,
Without love?
*(1st time to Verse 4:)*
*(2nd time to Verse 6:)*

Verse 4:
Instrumental Solo
*(To Verse 5:)*

Verse 6:
Where pistons keep on churnin'
And the wheels go 'round and 'round,
And the steel rails are cold and hard
For the miles that they go down.
Without love, where would you be right now,
Without love?
*(To Coda)*

# JUMP

Words and Music by EDWARD VAN HALEN, ALEX VAN HALEN,
MICHAEL ANTHONY and DAVID LEE ROTH

*Pre-chorus:*

see me stand-ing here? I got my back a-gainst the rec-ord ma-chine._____

**Elec. Gtr.** *(arr. for banjo)*

I ain't the worst that you've seen._____ Ah, can't you see what I mean?_

Ah, might as well_ jump._

*Chorus:*

**w/Synth. Riff,** *2 times*

_____ (Jump.)

{ Might as well jump._
{ Go a-head, jump._

# MAGGIE MAY

Words and Music by
ROD STEWART and MARTIN QUITTENTON

**Moderately** ♩ = 130

*Intro:*

1. Wake up, Mag-gie, I___ think I got some-thing to say to you.___ It's
2.3.4. *See additional lyrics*

*Optional picking pattern throughout*

late Sep - tem-ber and I real - ly should_ be back___ at___ school. I

*Interlude:*

**8va** *throughout*
**Mandolin** *(arr. for banjo)*

*mf*

1.2.3.4.

5.

*Outro:*

*Cont. rhy. simile*

Mag-gie,     I  wish I'd        nev - er seen_ your_ face.

I'll

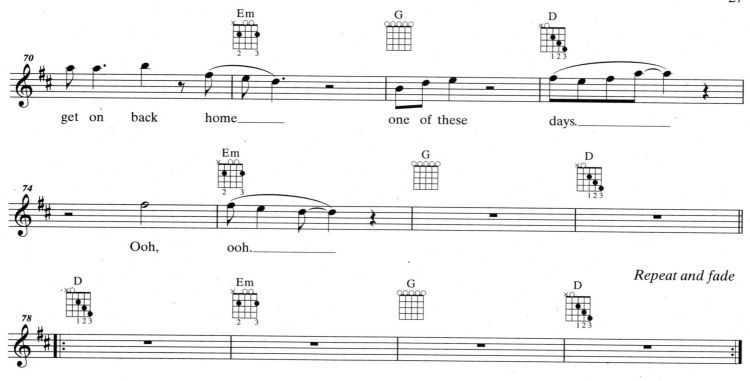

get on back home____ one of these days.____

Ooh, ooh.____

*Repeat and fade*

**Verse 2:**
The morning sun, when it's in your face,
Really shows your age.
But that don't worry me none,
In my eyes you're everything.
I laughed at all of your jokes,
My love you didn't need to coax.
Oh, Maggie, I couldn't have tried anymore.
You lead me away from home
Just to save you from being alone.
You stole my soul and that's a
Pain I can do without.

**Verse 3:**
All I needed was a friend
To lend a guiding hand.
But you turned into a lover and, mother,
What a lover, you wore me out.
All you did was wreck my bed,
And in the morning kick me in the head.
Oh, Maggie, I couldn't have tried anymore.
You lead me away from home
'Cause you didn't want to be alone.
You stole my heart,
I couldn't leave you if I tried.
*(To Guitar Solo 1:)*

**Verse 4:**
I suppose I could collect my books
And get on back to school.
Or steal my daddy's cue,
And make a living out of playing pool.
Or find myself a rock and roll band
That needs a helping hand.
Oh, Maggie, I wish I'd never seen your face.
You made a first-class fool out of me,
But I'm as blind as a fool can be.
You stole my heart
But I love you anyway.
*(To Guitar Solo 2:)*

# THE NIGHT THEY DROVE OLD DIXIE DOWN

Words and Music by
J. ROBBIE ROBERTSON

The Night They Drove Old Dixie Down - 3 - 1

The Night They Drove Old Dixie Down - 3 - 2

*Verse 2:*
Back with my wife in Tennessee,
One day she called to me,
"Virgil, quick come see,
There goes the Robert E. Lee."
Now, I don't mind choppin' wood,
And I don't care if the money's no good.
You take what you need and you leave the rest
But they should never have taken the very best.
*(To Chorus:)*

*Verse 3:*
Like my father before me,
I will work the land.
And like my brother above me,
Who took a rebel stand;
He was just eighteen, proud and brave,
But a Yankee laid him in his grave.
I swear by the mud below my feet,
You can't raise a Caine back up when he's in defeat.
*(To Chorus:)*

# TRUCKIN'

**Moderately fast ♩. = 114**

*Intro:*

Words by ROBERT HUNTER
Music by JERRY GARCIA,
BOB WEIR and PHIL LESH

*Chorus 1:*

*Cont. intro pattern simile*

*Cont. rhy. simile*

Truck - in',___ got_ my chips cashed_ in,___ keep truck -in',___ like the

*Optional roll pattern*

t i m t i m t i m t i m    t i m t i m t i m t i m    *Cont. rhy. simile*

doo - dah_ man.___ To - geth - er,___ more or less in_ line.___ Just keep truck-in' on.

Truckin'- 5 - 2

**𝄋 Bridge:**

Some - times_ the lights all shin - in' on me._

Oth - er_ times_ I can bare - ly_ see._

Late - ly it oc - curs to me,_ what a long,_

_ strange trip it's_ been._

*To Coda ⊕*

*Verses 3 & 4:*

3. What in the world ev - er be - came of Sweet Jane? She

4. Sit - tin' and star - in' out of the ho - tel win - dow, I'd

lost her spar - kle, you know she is - n't the same. She

got a tip they're gon - na kick the door in a - gain. I'd

Liv - in' on Reds, Vit - a - min C and co - caine,

like to get some sleep be - fore I trav - el. But if

all a friend can say is ain't it a shame.

you got a war - rant, I guess you're gon - na come in.

*Chorus 4 & 5:*

4. Truck - in' up to Buf - fa - lo, been think - in' you got to

5. Bust - ed down on Bour - bon Street, set up like a

mel - low slow. Takes time to pick a place to go, and

bowl - in' pin. Knocked down, it gets to wear - ing thin, they

just keep truck - in' on.

just won't let you be.

*Verse 5:*

5. You're sick of hang - in' a - round an' you'd like to trav - el. Get

# PAINT IT, BLACK

To match record key, Capo II

**Freely**

*Intro:*

Words and Music by
MICK JAGGER and KEITH RICHARDS

*Paint It, Black - 4 - 1*

*Outro:*

*Verse 3:*
I look inside myself and see my heart is black.
I see my red door, I must have it painted black.

*Bridge 3:*
Maybe then I'll fade away and not have to face the facts.
It's not easy facing up when your whole world is black.

*Verse 4:*
No more will my green sea go turn a deeper blue.
I could not foresee this thing happening to you.

*Bridge 4:*
If I look hard enough into the setting sun,
My love will laugh with me before the mornin' comes.
*(To Verse 5:)*

# STAIRWAY TO HEAVEN

**Slowly** ♩ = 72

Words and Music by
JIMMY PAGE and ROBERT PLANT

*Intro:*

1. There's a

*Verse 1:*

*Verses 2 & 3:*

there's still time to change the road you're on.
your stair - way lies on the whis - p'ring wind.

And it makes me won - der,

ahh.

Interlude:

hold throughout

Cont. in slashes

# SUNSHINE OF YOUR LOVE

Words and Music by
JACK BRUCE, PETE BROWN
and ERIC CLAPTON

**Moderately** ♩ = 114

*Sunshine of Your Love - 4 - 1*

# BANJO CHORD DICTIONARY

# A CHORDS

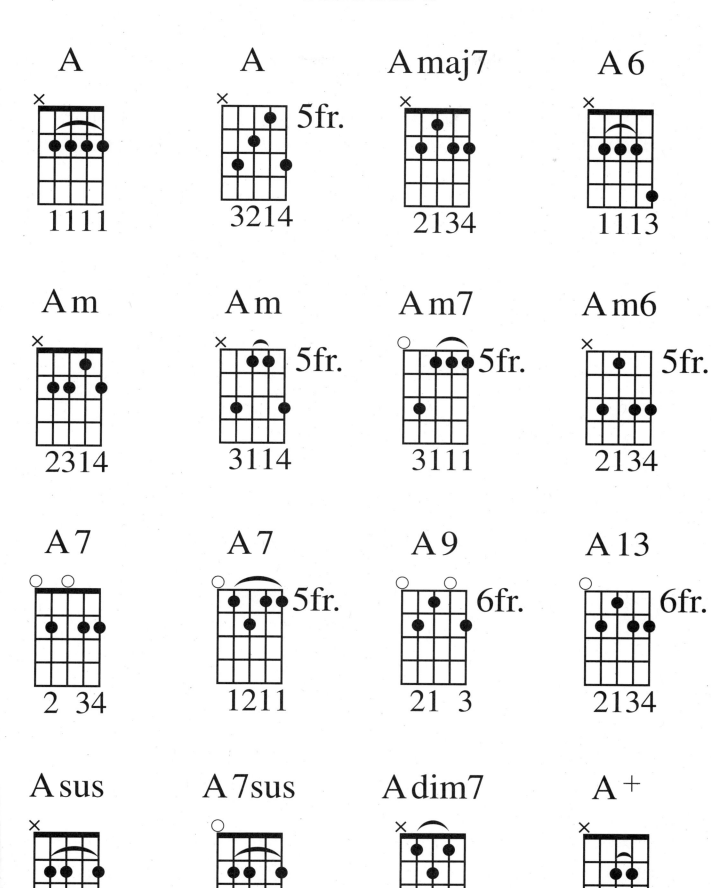

# B♭ (A♯) CHORDS*

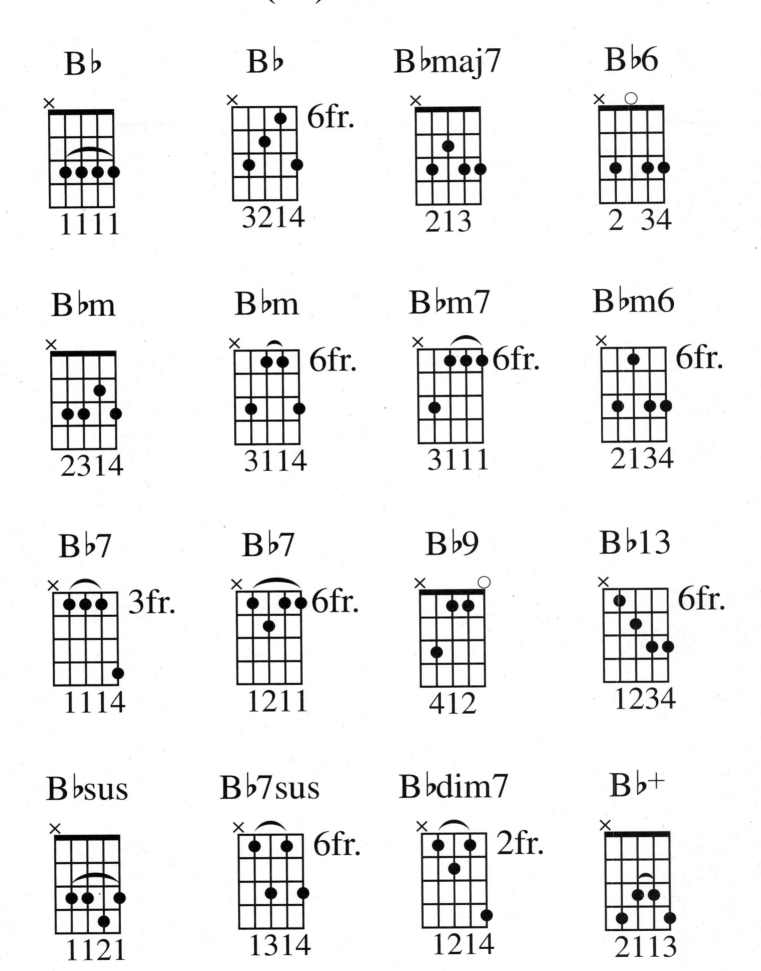

*B♭ and A♯ are two names for the same note.

# B CHORDS

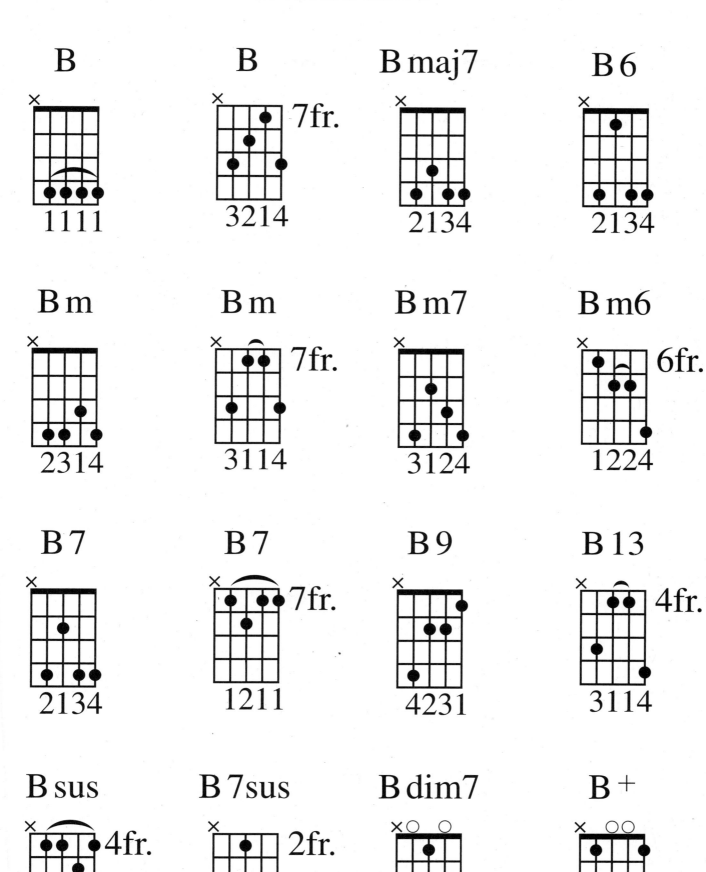

# C CHORDS

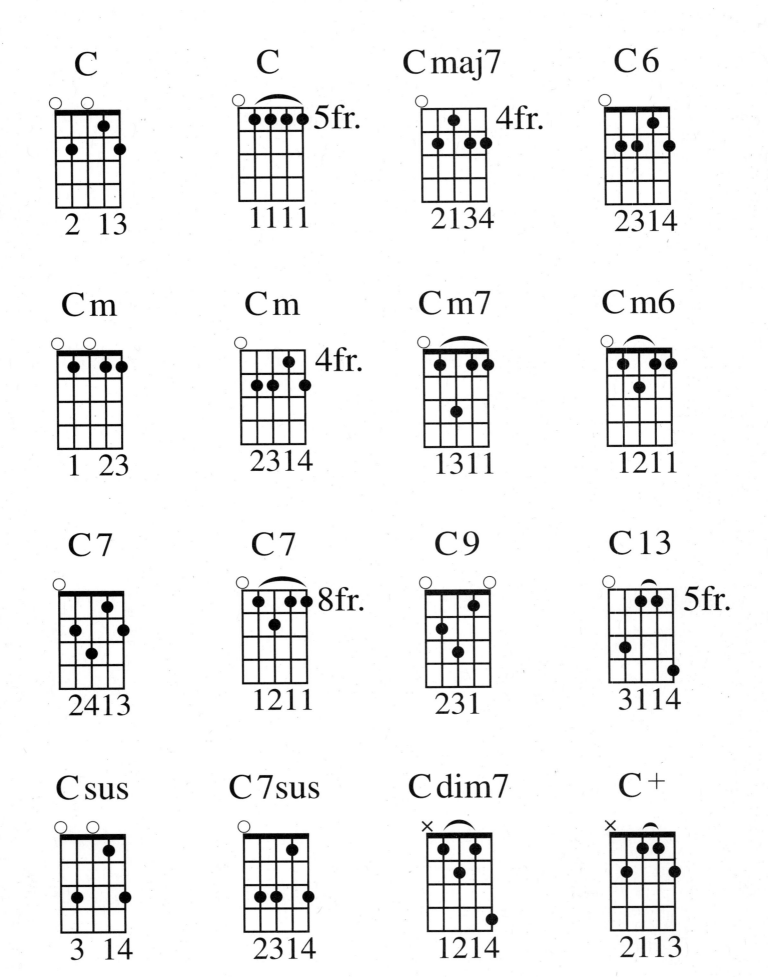

# C♯ (D♭) CHORDS*

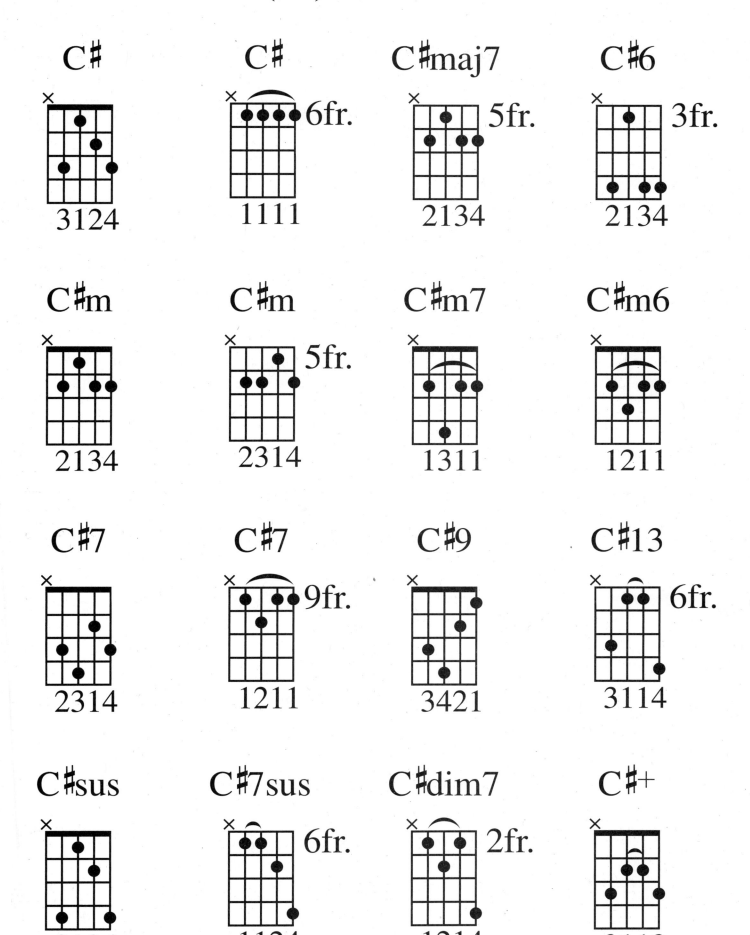

# D CHORDS

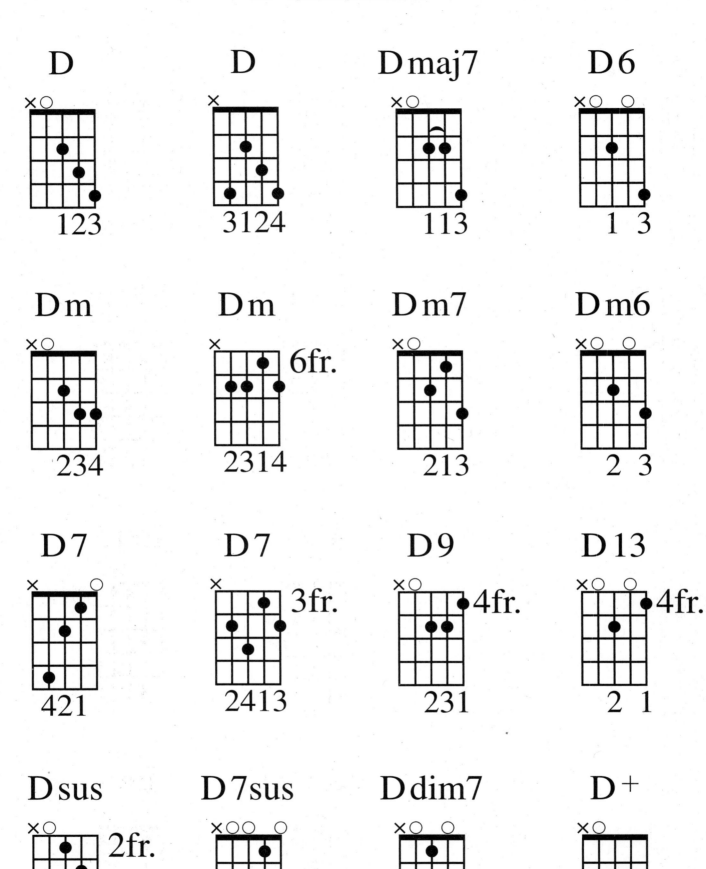

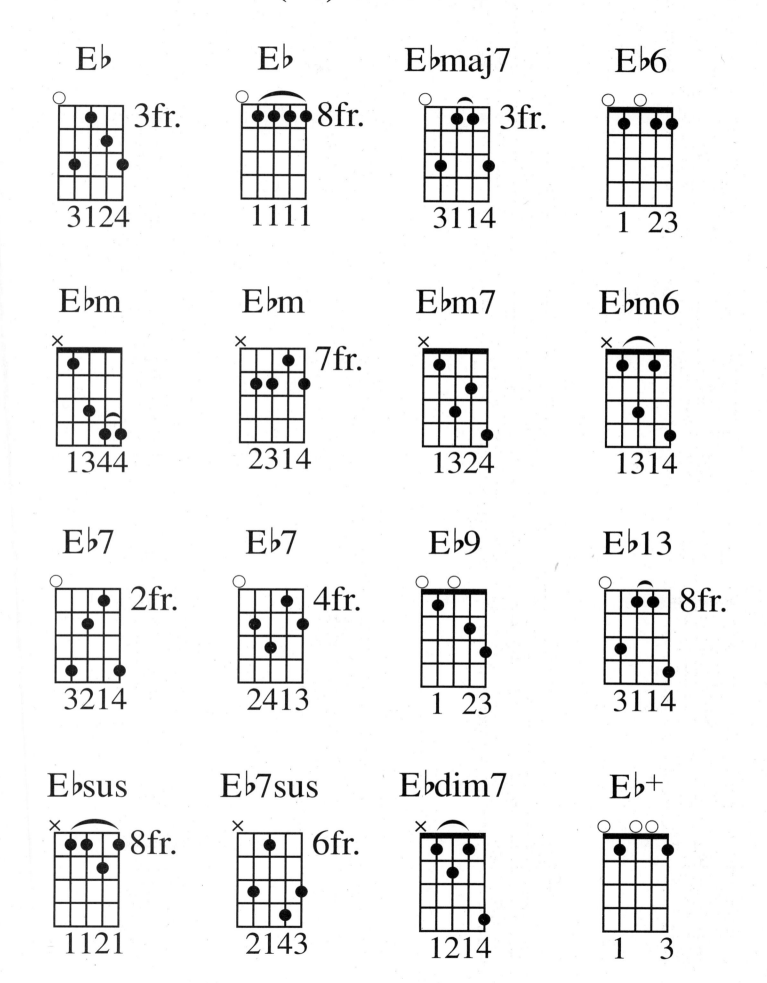

# E♭ (D♯) CHORDS*

*E♭ and D♯ are two names for the same note.

# E CHORDS

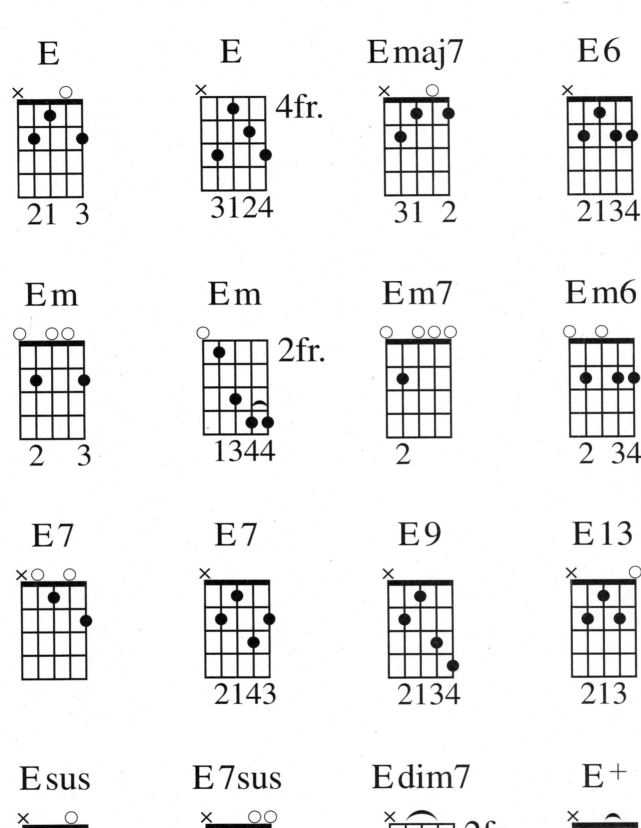

# F CHORDS

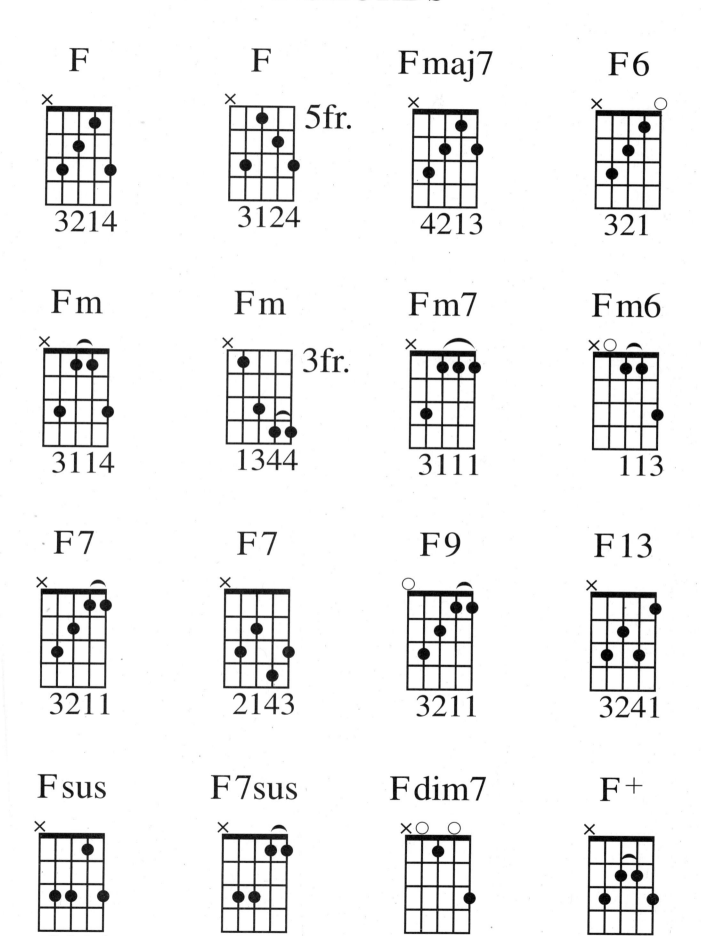

# F♯ (G♭) CHORDS*

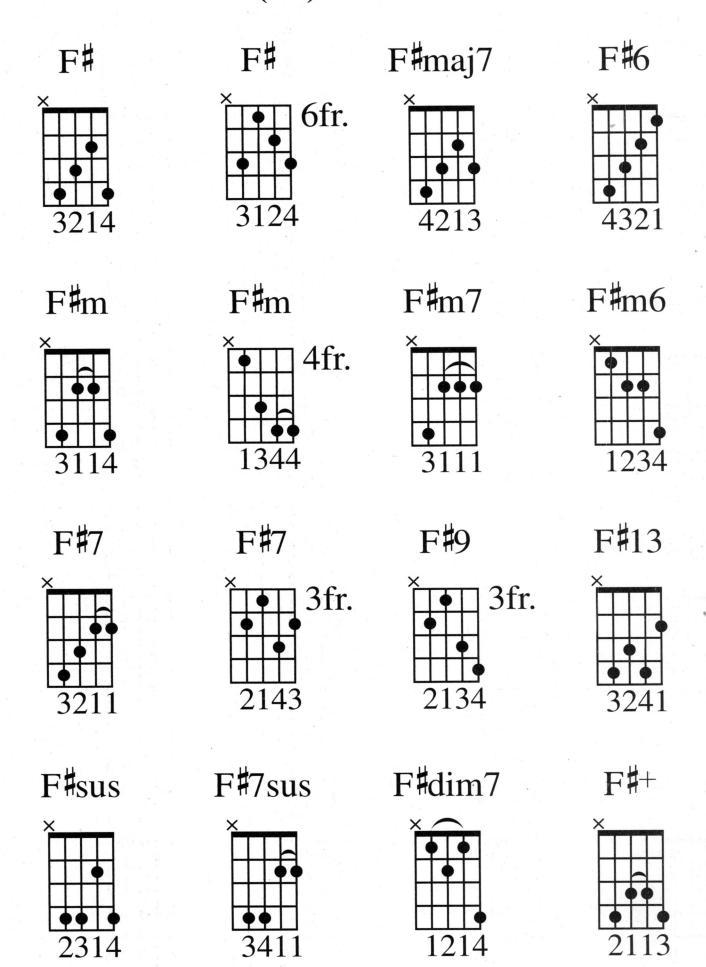

# G CHORDS

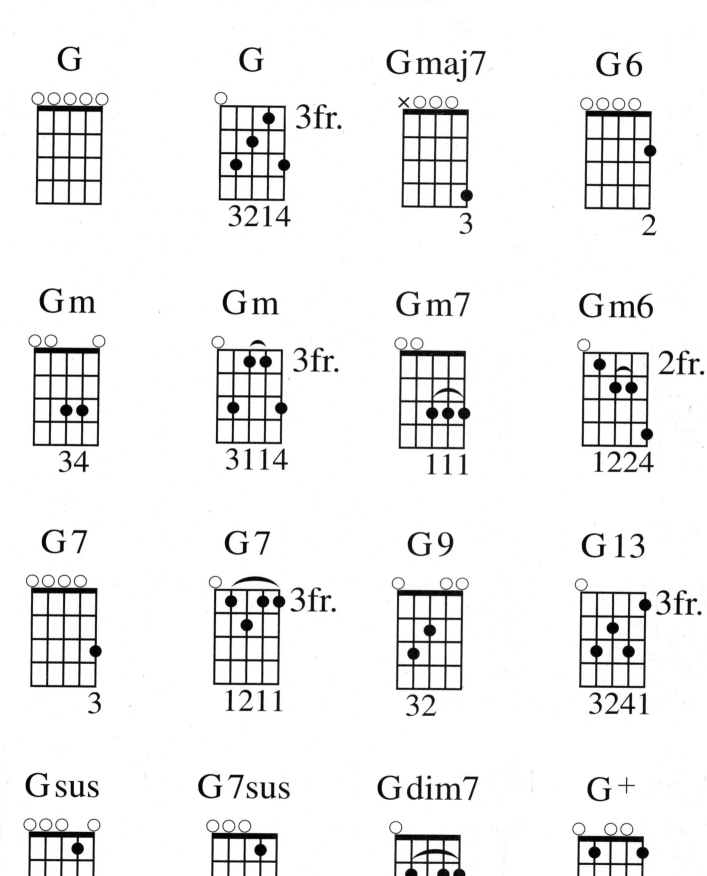

# Ab (G#) CHORDS*

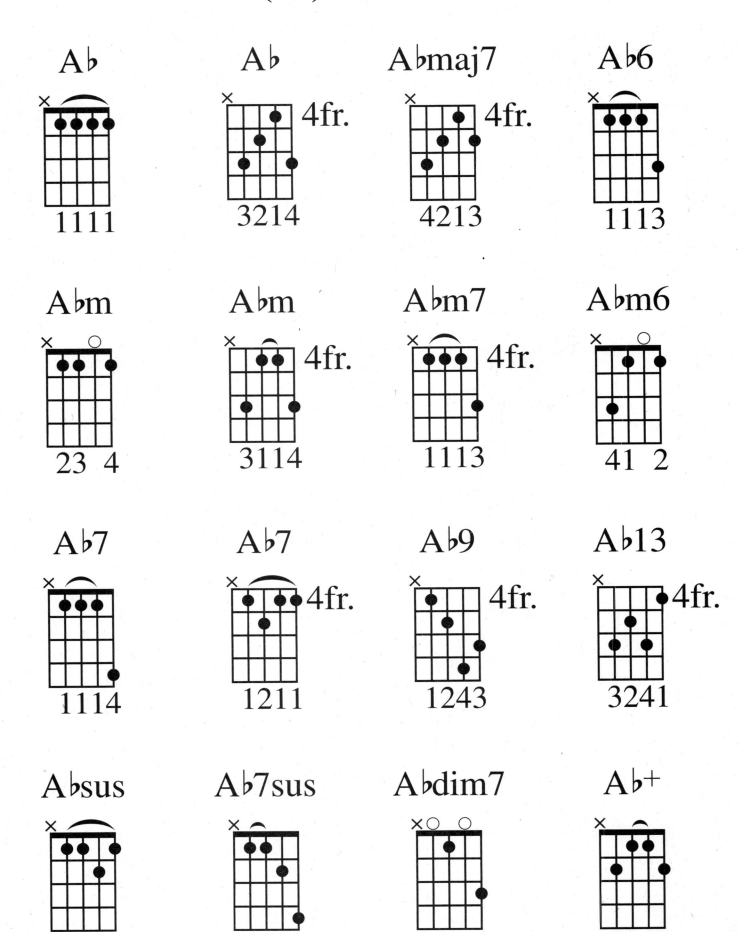

*Ab and G# are two names for the same note.